Pom

Dachshund

Beagle

Cocker Spaniel

Schipperke

Boston Terrier

Basenzi

A Ladybird Book
Series 682

*The dog has been man's companion
for thousands of years. Whether it is a pedigree
Welsh Corgi living in a Royal Palace, or a
humble mongrel of mixed breeds walking the roads
with a tramp without a home, a dog is
always a loyal friend, owning no other master
than the one to whom it belongs.*

*It has a long history in the service of man, and it
is this quality, bred in it over many
centuries, which makes it such a faithful and
devoted companion.*

A Ladybird book about
DOGS

by NANCY SCOTT

with illustrations by
B. H. ROBINSON

rom
John

Publishers Wills & Hepworth Ltd Loughborough
First published 1968   ©   *Printed in England*

The Beginning

Millions of years ago, before Man began life on this planet Earth, there lived a small carnivorous mammal known as MIACIS. Miacis had a body about twenty inches in length, with a tail as long as its body, but its legs were rather short, and it lived mainly in the trees. It was a carnivore, that is, it had teeth specially adapted for tearing and eating flesh, and claws on the ends of its toes for seizing and holding its prey.

Miacis was the ancient ancestor of the dogs and bears. It lived in the Oligocene period, some forty million years ago. At this time, mammals were fairly new to the Earth and were small.

As the years went by, Miacis developed into two larger types of animal — DAPHNEAUS and CYNODICTUS. Daphneaus developed into even larger animals until some became extinct, while others developed into the first bears.

But Cynodictus, shown in the foreground of the picture opposite, stayed a slender, long-bodied, short-legged animal, until the next period, the Miocene. In the Miocene period, there developed from Cynodictus three groups of dog-like animals. These were the first true dogs, the first members of the family CANIDAE.

One group became the ancestors of the hunting dogs of India and Africa, and the bush-dogs of South America. Another became the ancestors of the jackals and hyenas, and the third group developed into the foxes, wolves and dogs we know to-day.

In the foreground, Cynodictus— the ancestor of the modern dog

4

0 7214 0113 9

Cave-Man's Dog

Before the dog became man's companion, it was a wild creature, living and hunting in groups. Stone Age man was also a hunter, and among the animals that he hunted was the wild dog. Even as he pursued and killed it, he must have noticed and envied the remarkable hunting skills of those early canines, their speed, their keen sense of smell and their clever team work.

In time, the winters grew colder and longer. Food became difficult to obtain, so it may have happened that the hungry, wild dog, a hardy animal and himself unable to find sufficient fresh food, was drawn to the Stone Age man's camp by the savoury smells from the camp fire.

Stone Age man lived mainly in caves. Outside his cave was his midden, the place where he threw his rubbish. This rubbish included the bones and other unwanted scraps of the animals he had eaten. The wild dog soon learnt that the midden was an easy place on which to find tasty scraps of food. So the wild dog became a camp follower, and began to rely on man for his food supply.

This was probably about the time that primitive man took wild dogs, possibly as puppies, and trained them to work in his service as hunting dogs— using just those skills he had observed and admired. In this way the two hunters, man and dog, combined their efforts to the benefit of both.

In time, the wild dog became not only man's hunting partner, but also his tracker, his cave guardian and his daily companion.

6

Dogs of the Ancient East

By digging up old middens when excavating Stone, Bronze and Iron Age dwellings, archaeologists have discovered that the dogs of our early European ancestors were of a wolf-like breed.

However there were several distinct varieties of dog already known in other countries of the ancient world, but no-one has yet traced their early history. Nevertheless, despite this lack of knowledge, we do know that because of their skeletal structure and the formation of their teeth, they—like the European wolf-like dog—were all members of the CANIDAE family of mammals with a common ancestor in Cynodictus.

Carvings on ancient Egyptian and Chaldean temple walls and monuments show slender dogs of the greyhound type, and short-legged breeds of the terrier type. Large dogs of the mastiff breed were kept as guard dogs. They were tethered with thick collars and chains by day, and allowed to roam free in the courtyards at night.

Favourite dogs of the rich, upper-class Egyptians were often embalmed at death. Examples of these mummified dogs can be seen in most large museums. Egyptian children had model dogs as toys, just as children do to-day.

The Assyrians, Babylonians and Persians were also dog-owning people, and it is known from some ancient records that one of the early kings of Assyria kept large kennels of Mastiffs and Salukis for field-sports.

A Saluki of the ancient East

Dogs of Ancient Greece

Ancient Greece was another country in the East to have mastiff-like guard-dogs, Salukis and Greyhounds. In an illustration dating back to the sixth century B.C. a Greyhound with a feathered tail is shown, and it is believed that this was an ancestor of the modern Afghan Hound.

Another dog known to the Greeks at that time, but probably not to the Egyptians and other ancient eastern peoples, was a hound-type of dog with a rather pointed nose. This hound was similar to the Harrier of to-day, and was used as a 'scenting dog'. It was bred and trained to hunt the hare, not to catch it, but to track by smell and, working in a pack, to drive the hare into a net previously placed in position by the hunters.

This small harrier-type hound was a lively animal which could keep up the chase even when the day became stifling hot. Its sense of smell was extremely keen and sure, and needed to be because the smell of a hare quickly disappeared in the bare, dry sunny countryside. Its feet were firm and tough and well able to stand up to the long run over hard, rough mountainous ground.

But apart from the hounds bred for sport, and the Mastiffs as guard-dogs, the Ancient Greeks must certainly have kept dogs as pets, for many Ancient Greek vases show children playing with dogs which were obviously members of the household.

The Greek hunting dog

The Roman Fighting Dog

The Romans used the Mastiff in the gladiatorial shows they staged regularly in the amphitheatres throughout their Empire. But when they landed on the shores of Britain they were surprised to find that the people of this country also had Mastiffs larger and much fiercer than their own.

This mastiff-type dog must have been brought into Britain by the Celts who invaded this country long before the Romans came ashore. The Celtic tribes of Central Europe used Mastiffs in battle, and they were bred for strength and trained to be fierce fighters.

The Romans called their Mastiff breed, MOLLOSSUS. When they met this fiercer British Mastiff they gave it the name PUGNACES (fighting) MOLLOSI. Up to that time, the Roman Mollossus had been considered the greatest fighting dog in the world, but when pitted against the Pugnaces it was quickly overpowered. So until the end of the Roman occupation of Britain, regular supplies of Pugnaces were sent from this island to fight in the arenas all over the Roman Empire.

The Romans also had hounds for hunting, for guarding homes and flocks of sheep, and as pets. But when the Roman Empire fell to the attacks of the Barbarians, all written records of the smaller dogs disappeared. The Barbarians were only interested in the Pugnaces, the fighting dogs, because they were useful in battle.

The Roman fighting dog

The Tibetan Prayer-Dog

The Barbarians who destroyed the Roman Empire came from Central Asia, but beyond Central Asia are the countries of Tibet, Mongolia and China. In these far Asian countries were other distinct breeds of dog. One of these was the Tibetan Prayer-Dog, now known as the Tibetan Spaniel. This small dog was bred and trained in the monasteries to turn a prayer wheel. Prayers were written by the monks on pieces of parchment and put into a revolving box. It was the dog's duty to turn the box regularly so that the prayers were kept in motion. In this way the monks believed that their prayers were constantly being said.

This Spaniel also acted as a watch dog, sitting on the battlements of the monasteries and watching for any robbers who might approach the flocks of sheep and cattle owned by the monks.

Another use for this small dog was as a muff for the hands of the monks. It can be intensely cold in Tibet and the monasteries had no central-heating, so a monk would sit on cushions with his legs crossed and his hands folded inside his wide, open sleeves. Inside these sleeves, and curled up on his lap, would be a warm, soft little dog—a live hot water-bottle!

The Tibetan Spaniel spread from Tibet into China in this way. Each ruling dynasty at Lhasa had to pay annual tribute in money or goods to the Emperor of China at Peking, and the Spaniel formed part of this tribute. The smallest of these dogs were highly prized as pet dogs by the cultured Oriental courts of China.

The Lion Dog of Peking

The Chinese had a pug-type dog, and it is believed that the Tibetan Spaniel was crossed with this pug to produce the pug-nosed Pekinese.

In the first century A.D. the Emperor Ming T was converted to Buddhism. This was a moment ous event. It changed the whole course of Eastern history, and also changed the status of the little Chinese dog, the Pekinese.

The supreme symbol of Buddhism was the lion, but the Chinese of the capital city of China had never seen a real lion. One day someone looked down at the Emperor's small Pekinese dog and saw a resemblance to the pictures he had seen of a lion. From then on, the Pekinese grew in importance the idea of a lion faded into the background and the 'Lion Dog' took its place.

Because the Pekinese came to be regarded by the Chinese as sacred, the favourite dogs were given the rank of the highest mandarins, and lesser dogs were made dukes and princes. They had their own personal servants to attend them and slept on luxurious cushions.

It became the custom for the smallest dogs to be carried about in the voluminous sleeves of the long robes worn at Court by men and women These became known as 'sleeve dogs'. Later, smal Fekineses were specially bred for this purpose giving rise to yet another breed of dog, the Sleeve or Miniature Pekinese.

For hundreds of years the Pekinese was bred only in the Forbidden City of Peking. It was unknown outside China, and it wasn't until the downfall of the Manchu Emperors in the 19th century that the Pekinese became well-known.

A Pekinese 'Lion Dog

The Chow Dog

But if the Pekinese—the Lion Dog—was kep a hidden, secret dog, not so the Chow dog. Thi dog, with the blue tongue and thick fur coat, wa imported into North China many hundreds of year ago by the first men to come from Northern Asi These men, and their dogs, were the first to cros the great snow-covered waste-lands. They wer early explorers.

The Chow dogs were used mainly as sledg dogs as they were very hardy, and could live o almost any kind of food. But they were not onl used as working dogs; the Chinese found tha these imported dogs were good to eat, and fo centuries the Chow dog was well fattened with ric and was a part of the daily diet of the Chinese. Th thick, furry pelts of the Chow dog were exporte to other countries, including Britain.

In Mongolia, too, the Chow dog was fattened fo food, and its fur used for clothing. In fact, i Mongolia to-day there are still fur farms where th dogs are bred for their fur alone.

Its name comes from the use to which it wa put years ago—'chow' being the Chinese wo for food.

It is now known as the Chow Chow and is member of the Spitz breed of dog, all of whic originally came from the far North.

The hardy Ch

The Norman Hunting Dog

Wars, increased trade between countries, and the discovery of new lands by early explorers, meant that people began to move about more from one country to another. They took their dogs with them. This led to the mingling of the various early breeds. By the inter-breeding of different types, new breeds of dog developed, just as the mating of the Tibetan Spaniel with the Chinese Pug produced the Pekinese.

Up to the time of the Roman invasion there appeared to be only two types of dog in Britain—the wolf-like dog and the Mastiff brought in by the Celtic invaders. There may have been other types, but no-one can be sure.

No doubt other breeds of dog were brought over by later invaders and traders after the Romans left British shores, but that also is not known for sure. However, it *is* known that when the Normans invaded Britain in 1066, they brought with them their own special hunting dog, the Blood-hound. The Normans were keen hunters and their dogs were scenting dogs, able to follow the scent of the deer for many miles across open country or through dense forests.

The ordinary peasant was forbidden to hunt deer on Crown lands, and in order to stop him poaching, the keeping of large dogs in forest lands was also forbidden. Only dogs small enough to pass through an iron ring seven inches in diameter, and shepherd's dogs, were permitted.

A Norman and his hunting dogs

Dogs in Armour

The Norman kings and their followers used their dogs mainly for hunting. Many of these dogs wore wide collars fitted with metal studs and spikes. These were to protect the dog's neck, the most vulnerable part of an animal, from the attacks of wild animals. Sometimes the dogs wore even more protection than this, and were fitted with suits of armour carefully made to fit the animal's body. Samples of this medieval dog armour can be seen in certain European museums to-day. Only the most prized and favourite dogs of wealthy owners would be clothed in this way, of course, as such suits would have been expensive to make.

Throughout history, dogs have always been used in battle in some part of the world. Certainly the Britons used their fierce Mastiffs as fighters against the invading Romans, and from records we know that Henry VIII presented Emperor Charles V of Spain with four hundred war-dogs for use in his war against France, all of them fitted with wide, iron collars. Elizabeth I provided the Earl of Essex with a hundred war dogs for use in his campaign in Ireland; and Staffordshire Bull-terriers fought with the British boarding parties against the Spanish Armada.

A well-armoured hunting dog

The Scottish Deerhound

In Scotland, the chieftains had their own special hunting and game dog, the Rough Greyhound, now called the Deerhound. No Scottish castle was complete without several Rough Greyhounds in residence, and the great halls, with their high roofs and wide, open fire-places, made a fine setting for these large, handsome dogs.

So proud were the chieftains of their dogs that it was not unusual for great arguments to develop over the prowess of each individual dog. Sometimes these arguments became so heated that they led to pitched battles between the rival chieftains and their followers.

However, as the years went by, the Deerhound lost its popularity. It might have become completely extinct as a breed had not Sir Walter Scott kept a kennel of these dogs at Abbotsford, his home, and so helped to arouse fresh interest in them. Sir Edwin Landseer, the great 19th century painter, painted two of the Abbotsford Deerhounds. This also helped to awaken the awareness of dog-breeders to the danger facing this noble dog with such long history.

The Deerhound, and its cousin the Irish Wolfhound, are both descended directly from the Celtic dogs brought into Britain long before the Romans arrived.

Handsome Deerhounds in a castle

The Racing Greyhound

Greyhound racing is an ancient sport. When setting a Greyhound after a hare, we are in fact following a custom which goes back to the Ancient Egyptians of five thousand years ago.

The Greyhound was bred for its great speed and keen sight, and to hunt small animals on the desert plains. It was also used to provide sport for the local people—the dogs being raced one against the other, usually chasing live bait. This practice, now referred to as greyhound coursing, spread throughout Europe and eventually to this country. However, to set one animal to chase another is no longer considered 'sport' by many people.

Greyhound track racing is a very new sport by comparison, as it dates back only to about 1920. The idea came from America. Basically this form of racing uses the same natural instinct of a dog—to give chase—but instead of live bait being chased, a dummy hare is used which is attached by an arm to an electric trolley. The trolley travels round the track at a speed which is always just a little ahead of the leading dog. The Greyhounds used for this sport are all specially trained and know exactly what they must do from the moment they are put into the pens at the start of the race. The length of each race is strictly regulated so that the dogs are not overstrained.

A racing Greyhound

The Bull-Baiting Dogs

Years ago, people thought it great sport to set one animal against another, sometimes dog against dog, or dogs against lion, dogs against bears, or even dogs against bulls. Often these fights were to the death, but usually the dogs were trained to pin down their adversary in some way.

One day, a certain rich earl saw an infuriated bull being chased and tormented by dogs. He thought it great sport and decided that this should become an annual sport for the entertainment of himself and the local people. He gave a part of his castle meadow rent free to the local butchers for their use on the condition that, six weeks before Christmas every year, they provided a bull which would be baited and chased by trained dogs.

The dog chosen to be used in the new 'sport' was a stocky terrier breed which had been in England for many hundreds of years. In time the terrier's face became malformed by the way it was taught to grip with its nose and lower lip. As successive pups were born, they inherited the strange flat-faced appearance of their bullbaiting parents and a new breed called the Bulldog was created.

In time, certain people decided this was an extremely cruel sport—for dog and bull—and they agitated in Parliament to get it banned by law. After a long struggle they succeeded. These people were the founder members of the Society for the Prevention of Cruelty to Animals, now granted a Royal Charter and known as the R.S.P.C.A.

Foxhounds

Foxhunting as a sport became organised and popular in the 14th century. At that time most of the followers of the hunt went on foot, but gradually more and more of them took to riding horseback. As the years went by, horses became faster, and so a faster breed of hunting hound was necessary.

Not only did the dog's speed need to be greater, his sense of smell needed to be keener to enable him to keep to the scent-trail over land treated with artificial manures and chemical sprays and through air polluted by the fumes of oil and petrol.

The earlier hunting hounds in Britain had been of two main types—the northern Hounds with slim bodies and long legs, best suited to hilly and mountainous country, and the southern Hounds which had much heavier, thicker-set bodies and shorter legs.

By selective breeding between these two types of hounds, plus other lesser-known breeds of hunting hound, there evolved the splendid modern Foxhound combining the speed and agility of the northern breeds and the stocky stamina of the southern, and also possessing a good nose for the scent of the fox, and a loud bark.

A loud bark is necessary for this type of hunting. A pack of hounds in full cry flushes out the lurking fox and guides the following mounted riders in the direction of the chase. Many people regard this sport as a cruel one.

Foxhounds and the hu

Dogs of the Arctic

The Husky dog, pulling a sledge over the snowy wastes of the Arctic, is well-known to all who have read about the early explorers of the Far North.

The name 'Husky' covers several breeds of dog which came from the frozen north and which, like the Chow Chow, have been used for centuries as sledge dogs.

The largest of all the working sledge dogs is the Alaskan Malamute, a breed originally developed by a tribe of Eskimos, the Malamute or Innuit tribe. The way they bred the Malamute was simple — by the survival of the fittest. The climate in that area of Alaska has always been hard, and the early dogs had to learn to survive on the smallest amount of food and to be able to stand up to the lowest temperatures.

In addition to being big and hardy, the Alaskan Malamute is an extremely strong dog and can pull four times its own weight, its weight being about ninety to one hundred pounds.

In the Canadian backwoods and the North West Territories, the true Husky, or a half-breed dog of the Husky type, is still used as a sledge dog by many people—trappers, explorers, lumberjacks, doctors, priests, Canadian Mounted Police, and any others who need to travel over the snow-covered countryside, for the dog-drawn sledge is still the most reliable way in which to travel safely over vast snow-bound areas.

A Husky dog

The Sheep-dog

Many breeds of dog have been used as sheep-dogs throughout history, but perhaps the most elegant and intelligent of them all is the Border Collie.

It is a descendant of the dogs of the Arctic, the Huskies, Elkhounds and Samoyeds. Elkhounds can be traced back to four or five thousand years before Christ, and skeletons of these dogs have been discovered in Norway by archaeologists. Many years ago the Norwegians settled in Scotland and the Western Isles, so there is little doubt that the Border Collie originally came over with the Norsemen.

In training these dogs to round up and bring in large flocks of sheep, man is using the old hunting instinct inherent in every dog. All dogs will chase and round up sheep and other cattle. Even a town bred dog, whose ancestors for centuries have never known the necessity to hunt for their food, will instinctively give chase and round up farm animals if not kept under strict control. But an untrained dog's instinct then leads it to attack and kill, whereas a sheep-dog is taught to chase, round up skilfully and bring in the sheep, but *never* to attack them.

It works in partnership with the shepherd, and although it is trained to be obedient to the signals of the shepherd, it is not a blind, slave-like obedience, for the best sheepdogs are among the most intelligent of the canines, and really understand what they are doing. They understand so well that they can, when necessary, work alone,

The Carriage Dog

The ancestors of this unique, spotted dog are unknown, and no-one seems to know how it got its name 'Dalmatian'. Dalmatia is a province of Yugoslavia, but no attractive, spotted dogs are found in that district to-day. Some time in the distant past, several breeds of dog must have been crossed to produce this mixture of Pointer, Great Dane, and hunting dog of Bengal. The Bengal hunting dog is now extinct, but it is known to have been a spotted type.

Before the 17th century, the Dalmatian was used in Europe as a hunting dog, but from the mid-17th century onwards it became increasingly popular as a guard dog for coach travellers. These long-legged dogs had no trouble in keeping up with a coach as it bowled and rattled along the poor roads of pre-motor vehicle days. Their large size, easily seen coats, coupled with their natural hunting instinct that made them keep up the pursuit, deterred many a footpad or highwayman from holding up an approaching coach.

So useful and well-known did the Dalmatian become as a coach-guard, that soon people were keeping it to accompany their smaller, private carriages. Usually two dogs were kept, as they worked better in pairs.

Even when the roads became a little safer from the attacks of highwaymen, the Dalmatian still kept its popularity as a carriage dog. By that time it had become a status symbol, and no family of high social standing would think of riding out without its aristocratic-looking carriage dogs running behind.

Guard dogs run with the carriage

The Decorative Poodle

The attractive Poodle can be traced back to Germany where for centuries it was known as the Water Spaniel. The French made use of it as a gundog, particularly for duck shooting, as it is one of the finest water retrievers. The custom of clipping the coat into patterns began for several practical reasons: the weight of the water in the thick uncut fur would have dragged the dog below the surface. At first the Water Spaniel was clipped all over, but later only the coat behind the ribs was cut, leaving the 'mane' to protect the heart and lungs. 'Bracelets' of hair on the legs were left as a guard against underwater hazards.

During the reign of Louis XVI, the Poodle became the pet of fashionable France, and so began the many and varied clipping designs. 'Poodle Barbers', along the banks of the Seine, did a busy trade pandering to the whims of the French aristocrats.

The Cavalier Prince Rupert, in the reign of Charles I, owned a Poodle named Boye. This Poodle was said to have supernatural powers, and one writer of the time regretted the opportunity Boye had of conversing with the king's children 'lest he taught them to swear'. Another writer published detailed accounts of Boye as a church-goer. 'He conducted himself most Popishly, and was never late for prayers.' Boye fell in battle at Marston Moor.

The name 'poodle' comes from its modern German name Pudel. The word 'pudeln' means 'to splash in water'.

Modern War Dogs

Throughout history, dogs have been used in time of war, but in early centuries their use was mainly as actual fighters alongside man. A large dog trained to attack was every bit as deadly as a sword or spear. Then came the invention of the gun, and dogs were no longer needed as fighters. But they still have their uses in wartime.

Suitable dogs are trained at the War Dogs School, and it is amazing the things a well-trained dog can do. It can become a messenger dog, slipping silently through enemy lines, passing unnoticed down the street of an occupied town, or scaling mountain ranges, carrying a coded message hidden in its collar or among its thick fur. It can lead a reconnaissance patrol, using its natural scenting instincts to give immediate warning of the presence of an enemy. It can detect mines, find wounded soldiers and airmen, carry small supplies of ammunition or food to places out of reach of other transport, and act as a guard or patrol dog.

There are many stories told of the heroism of dogs in time of war, stories which prove how great is the understanding and intelligence of the dog. Usually a dog will shrink from exploding fireworks and howl loudly with pain if its pad is trodden on. Yet in wartime, dogs have been known to keep still and silent with shells exploding all around them; even when injured they have not whimpered, knowing that to do so would be to give away the presence of their handlers to the enemy.

A war dog in World War I

Mountain Rescue Dogs

It is not only in wartime that a dog can be used in the service of man. The St. Bernard dog is regularly used for rescue work high in the Alps where snow lies several feet deep for most of the year.

The St. Bernard has a long history, but not under this name. It began life as the Roman Mollossus, and was used by Roman soldiers when travelling over the Alps to conquer other countries. A dog will never walk into deep snow, so Mollossus was sent ahead of the first party of troops — the theory being that where the dog would tread, man also could tread in safety.

One of the passes built over the Alps by the Romans was later chosen by some monks as the place in which to build a Hospice, and at first they also used the Mollossus as their guide. This Hospice was founded by a man named Bernard de Menthon and he named it after St. Nicholas. When he died, the Hospice was renamed the Hospice of the Great St. Bernard.

One of the main tasks of these monks was to help lost or stranded travellers, and about the year 1665 they decided to use dogs in this work. They chose for training, large dogs with short-haired coats and the right temperament to stand up to the blizzards and sudden, fierce storms that arise in the Alps.

At first these dogs were called Hospice dogs and Alpine Mastiffs, but gradually they became known by the name of the monastery, St. Bernard at which they worked.

St. Bernard dogs in the Alps

Guide Dogs

At the end of the First World War, the German Government gave to each of its war-blinded soldiers a fully-trained guide-dog, and so out of the bitterness of war came one of the most useful ways of using the abilities of the dog. The idea quickly spread to other countries.

Nearly all the dogs trained are females, because males are too easily tempted to quarrel with other dogs — and not all breeds of dog can be trained. Most of the guide-dogs are now Alsatians (German Shepherd-dogs), or Labrador Retrievers, although Border Collies, Keeshonds, Boxers, some cross-breeds, and (in the U.S.A.) Dobermann Pinschers, are also trained if they have the right temperament for the job.

A dog begins its training as a puppy, when it is house-trained and taught to walk on a lead. Then follow four to five months further training before a dog is ready to meet its new owner. The blind person has then to learn how to rely on the dog which in future will act as his eyes, leading him along crowded pavements, safely across busy roads, and onto trains and buses. It takes a month of training at the Guide-dog Training School for owner and dog to learn to work in partnership, and during this training period the blind person also learns how to care for his dog.

Training guide dogs is one of the good causes to which people gladly give their money.

A Labrador Retriever and an Alsatian
(at rear) being trained as guide-dogs

Police Dogs

The dogs used to assist the Police in their work have a very strict training. Each dog has one particular policeman to obey. This policeman is known as the 'handler', and each dog must learn complete obedience to the orders of its own handler.

These dogs are used for two main purposes — to guard important buildings and to track and capture criminals. Every person has his or her own particular smell, and will leave a trace of this smell on everything touched. If a trained police dog smells an item of clothing which has been worn by a person, it will follow the track of that person for miles. If, when trying to escape, the criminal throws away a weapon, or buries some stolen property, the tracker-dog will find it by the personal smell.

A policeman cannot easily or quickly search thick bushes or push through dense undergrowth, so he sends his dog, and many a hidden criminal has been flushed out of hiding by the growl of a dog. This growl brings the handler to the spot; but the dog will do no more than growl until it is given further orders from its handler. If the criminal tries to run away, the dog may be told to go after him, and if that happens then the dog will try to bring the man down by dragging on his clothes, gripping his arm, or even tripping him up.

Although Alsatians are the dogs most used by the Police to-day, other breeds have been and still are used. One of the most famous police dogs was Ben, a black Labrador. He made over one hundred arrests.

An Alsatian grabs a suspect

Toy Dogs

Big dogs, such as the St. Bernard, which may weigh as much as two hundred and ten pounds, and very tall dogs like the Irish Wolfhound, are not at all suitable for the average home, so many people choose a miniature breed, known generally as a Toy dog. A Toy dog is one which has been bred down in size from a larger breed.

The smallest is the tiny Mexican Chihuahua which rarely weighs more than four pounds, and stands about nine inches high. This little dog is descended from the Aztec sacred dog. The Aztecs settled in Mexico in the 13th and 14th centuries and these sacred dogs, then known as the Teechichi, were bred and fattened as a sacred dish for the Aztec high priests. Some were also kept as pets.

The Papillon with its ears shaped like butterfly wings, also comes from Mexico, although it is believed to be of European origin.

The Pug has been a favourite Toy dog in Britain for more than two hundred years. No-one knows how it came by the queer name 'Pug'.

Smallest of all the British terriers is the silky-haired Yorkshire Terrier. It was created as a new breed about a century ago from the Scottish, Old English Black-and-Tan and Clydesdale Terriers.

Toy Dogs were not originally bred as dogs for the smaller home. Although some were bred specially as pets, most of them were bred as ratters, and were kept in homes to chase and kill the rats and other small vermin. All Toy Dogs can be fierce, aggressive and noisy fighters if given the chance.

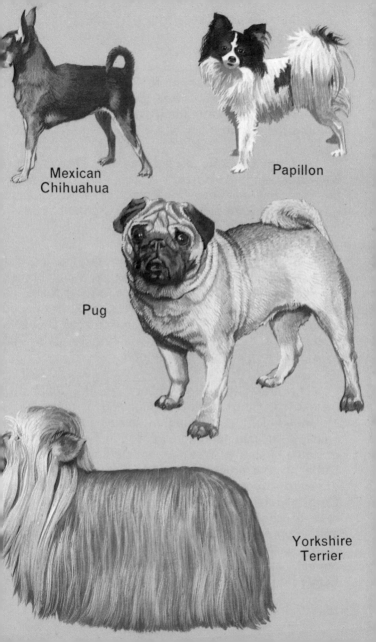

Mexican
Chihuahua

Papillon

Pug

Yorkshire
Terrier

Royal Dogs

The King Charles Spaniel is named after Charles II who, according to Pepys the great 17th century diarist, spent more time playing with his little dogs than attending to his business or running the country.

A great favourite of the Russian Tzarist Court was the elegant Borzoi. It was bred for wolf-hunting, but because most of these dogs were owned by the nobility, many fine kennels ceased breeding after the Russian Revolution.

The Clumber Spaniel is the largest of the English sporting Spaniels — all Spaniel breeds were once used for hunting or sport. It takes its name from Clumber Park where it was developed about 1770. Some of the best dogs of the 20th century are descended from the fine kennels kept by King George V at Sandringham.

The endearing Welsh Corgi is the main dog resident at Court to-day. It has had a long history as an efficient cattle dog in Wales. Although so small, it is able to round up and drive large herds of cattle, using a heel-nipping method to keep the cattle on the move. In the days when cattle were driven on foot many miles to market, the nimble Corgi would bring a straggler into line with the rest of the herd by running behind the animal and nipping its heels. Even to-day, a domestic Corgi will suddenly nip the heels of another animal, or its own master or mistress, if some happening arouses this instinct within it.

King Charles Spaniel

Borzoi

Clumber
Spaniel

Welsh Corgi

Irish Setter

Boxer

Old English
Sheepdog

Scottie

Shetland Sheepdog

Staffordshire
Bull Terrier

Irish Terrier